Hope and Joy Glutzman

Connie 12/07

Jamie Koch

Gulf Coast Memory Scrapbook

by
Connie Heitzmann & Janie Koch

A Pictorial Journey of Hope and Healing

Come take a sentimental journey of the Gulf Coast Critter Queen's Memory Scrapbook. There are many places to visit and maybe even a few things to be learned about the beautiful Mississippi Gulf Coast. The beauty abound is reflected through the talented and abundant artists on the Coast. Through their eyes you will see the reason so many people would not think of calling any place else "home." So come enjoy the adventure with "Freckles the Firefly" into the picturesque gallery of the *Gulf Coast Memory Scrapbook*.

DEDICATION

This book is dedicated to the Heitzmann family; Bob, Matt and Ashley.
Also dedicated to the Koch family; Frank, Thomas, Sara, John and Bill,
and all our artist friends who contributed to this rare and special book.
A special dedication goes to the many volunteers who came to help us in our time of need.
Thank God for our blessings.

Special thanks to the following angels for their time, talent, help, and encouragement:

Sheri Armstrong
Stanisluvi Babenko
Linda Beauregard
Lisa Bouis
Janet Buras
Eddie Coleman
Bonita Favre
Betsy Gagnet
Kay Gleber
Charles Gray
Suzi Hand
Ames Kergosien
Bill Koch
Martha Merrigan

Reg & Margie Morkin
Ken Murphy
Vicki Niolet
Mary Perkins
Karen Phillips
Sarah Richie
Jan Rutherford & Family
Betty Stechmann
Michael Tracey
Alex Treutel
Angelyn Treutel
Bragg Williams
Tish Haas Williams
Rachel Winters

Alice Moseley Folk Art Museum
All Disney Friends
Hancock County Chamber of Commerce
Hancock County Library
Hancock County Historical Society
Lynn Meadows Discovery Center
NASA - Stennis Space Center

Special thanks to our guest artists for their talented contributions:

Janie Koch, Co-Author and Artist/Illustrator

Front cover artwork by Karen Renz & Janie Koch
Back cover artwork by Janie Koch

Guest Artists:

Barbara Brodtmann
Kathe Calhoun
Dot Copeland
Sylvia Corban
Margaret Heitzmann
Anne Kearney
Rickey Lewis
Janise McCardle

John McDonald
Tricia McDonald
Tazewell Morton
Alice Moseley
Tim Moseley
Karen Renz
Betty Stechmann
Linda Theobald

Winters Publishing
P.O. Box 501
Greensburg, IN 47240
www.winterspublishing.com
800-457-3230

Cover and Text Page Graphic Design by Rachel Winters

Printed in South Korea

ISBN-10: 1-883651-30-1   ISBN-13: 978-1-883651-30-5

Library of Congress Control Number: 2007932940

Waveland, Mississippi is our "Soft Shell Crab Capital of the World." People come from many places to pick up crabs at night so they can enjoy this wonderful adventure.

Many tales have been told,
about a pirate house with hidden gold.
His house sat on the beach you see,
waiting there for you and me.
A story of the stolen bell,
has quite an adventure for some to tell.
The bell is back to our delight,
back where it belongs, and this is right.
Without the mystery of Jean Lafitte,
our Gulf Coast Pirate would not be complete.

Laissez les bons temps rouler

"Let The Good Times Roll"

All enjoy the southern breeze,
On the Shoo-Fly of a Live Oak Tree.

Notice the Spanish-Moss that hangs from the limbs,
Like an old grey beard off Grandpa's chin.

The Pot of Gold's at the End of the Rainbow in Bay St.Louis

a. Moseley
Tim Moseley

Bay Saint Louis, MS - A Place Apart

Freckles reminds us of the nickname "Bay Ratz" started for the Bay Saint Louis young people back in the late 50's.

Papa Trap welcomes all
Bay Ratz, friends big and tall.
Sunshines then Trapanis shared this space,
A different time but the same place -
Food and friends are great by the way
So come on down to the Bay!

"The Palm House" – Childhood Home of the "Critter Queen"
Bay Saint Louis, Mississippi

Ladner's Seafood on Hancock St. was the place where friends would meet. On Friday nights, all would come to enjoy Slim and Kitty 'fore the day was done.

Yea! Great fun at the Lipton Races.

Bay Waveland Yacht Club
Bay Saint Louis, Mississippi

ROUND TRIP
Hummingbird
Express
0202401

The roar of the trains coming through our town
Called "all aboard" from the Mississippi Sound.
Come one, come all to see and hear
The many faces from far and near.

Magnolias and Mockingbirds grace our town
Small and quaint with friends around.
You'll know us from our smiling faces
Passing by our small town places.

I wasn't born in Mississippi, but I got here as soon as I could.

Henderson Point
Mississippi

Our 1967 St. Joseph Academy Camellia Queens celebrated monthly at Annie's Restaurant. (Excitement on our 40th reunion)

Martin's Hardware in the "Pass"
is a friendly place indeed.
You'll find paint and nails and good advice
for all your handyman needs.
Thanks for getting back in shape
To help us on our way
We won't forget since '32
you've been around to stay.

Inn at the Pass
Pass Christian

Mallini Bayou
(Boisedore Bayou)

Mallini Bayou with its peaceful waters,
Golden Woods with little otters.
A palette of color displays its critters
For all to enjoy, please don't litter.

Pass Christian
Birthplace of Southern Yachting

St. Paul's Catholic Church
Established 1847

The beaches are littered with painted trash cans, designed by great artists to clean up the sand.

Waiting for a fish to eat
Is our friend Pelican Pete.
Watching Sails of SSC
Summer Camp is the place to be!

Camp Saint Stanislaus

Long Beach Harbor
Long Beach, Mississippi

"Boggsdale"
A lovely Beach Estate
Long Beach, Mississippi

Friendship Oak Motto
I am called
'Friendship Oak.'

Those who enter my shadow are supposed to remain friends through all their lifetime, no matter where fate may take them in years.
— sophomore class 1959

FRIENDSHIP OAK

Karen Anne Perry

"Gulfport's Beachfront Katrina Survivors"
Thanks, Vrazel's, for coming back!

Ship Island Excursion Boat offers a nice day trip to discover Fort Massachusetts.

200/1000   "All 'dat Jazz"   Tazewell

"All 'dat Jazz"
Beach Critters

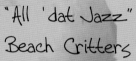

Our snow cones are
flavored,

and they're such a
treat.

They're cool and
delicious

and oh so sweet.

BLESSING OF THE FLEET

IN REMEMBRANCE

MS CONNIE

Ms Janie

The ceremony begins with
the dropping of an evergreen wreath
into the sound in
remembrance of fishermen
who have been lost at sea.
Each boat is given a blessing,
asking for a safe
and prosperous fishing season.

Seafood here is the best in the land.
You are hooked once your feet touch our sand.
Biloxi Bacon's the treasure you seek,
casting the net away from your feet.
Mullet is the "Catch of the Day."
After you're done, you'll play, play, play.

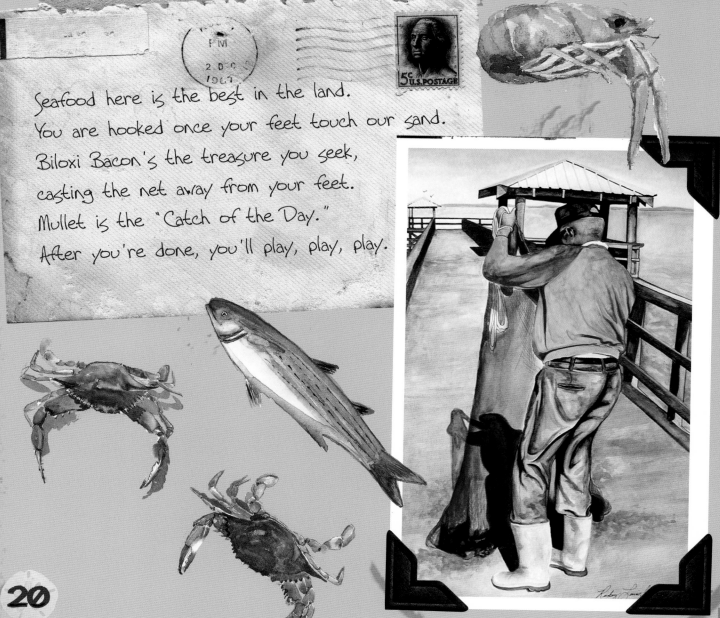

**CRITTER QUEEN-
O.L.G. CRAB FEST**

CRAB
ROULÉ
IN THE BAY

Greatest chefs, food, music
and fun can be found at our
Annual Crab Festival
at O.L.G.

Our Lady of the Gulf
Annual Crab Festival
Gene Taylor ~ Crab Races

Welcome to
"Pascagoula Critter
River Tours"

Cat Island Light House

Biloxi Light House

Great Wildlife on the Beautiful Mississippi Sound

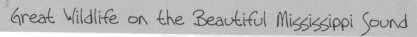

Cat Island

Horn Island

Ship Island

Biloxi's Mardi Gras and Jazz Society

Memories of our friends from Carlow, Ireland and our beautiful Gulf Coast.

St. Patrick's Day Parade

23

St. Joseph's Chapel

Cedar Point – Bay Saint Louis

"The New Convent Follies." What fun!

Our Ocean Springs, Mississippi is artsy, pristine, and just plain beautiful.

One of *the oldest cities in the* United States, Ocean Springs, was founded in 1699 by French explorer Pierre Le Moyne d'Iberville.

HOME SWEET F.E.M.A. HOME

WE ARE STAYIN

Little white boxes here and there,
FEMA RV's were everywhere.
Home Sweet Home is where you stay
It doesn't matter. All is ok.

25

Diamondhead Yacht Club

Go Brett

Hancock County
Library
Welcome to the
'hub' of Hancock
County, Mississippi

NASA

Stennis Space Center

(America's largest rocket test complex)

Before you get to the moon you have to go
through Hancock County, Mississippi.

The Koch Family's Hurricane Katrina Story
By Janie Koch

We live two and a half miles from the beach, and during Hurricane Camille, in 1969, there was no water in our house. I have lived either in or next door to the house I was raised in most of my life. Eudora Welty, the famous author from Jackson, Mississippi, said something about folks from the south stay in one place, so they can watch life unfold around them. This rings true around here.

About 9:30 on Monday morning, August 29, 2005, we had just eaten breakfast, and thought we had survived the worst of the winds. A lot of trees down, but none on our house, thank God. When I heard water running, I thought, "How could that be?" We had no electricity to run the pump on the well. The electricity had gone out about four hours earlier. Then we noticed water on the floor. It was coming into the house through the sides of the back door, making a splashing noise when it hit the water on the floor. We looked outside and saw that the water was about a foot deep. We started running around the house trying to put things up on tables, beds, anything to keep them dry. When we came out of the bedroom, we noticed that the water on the outside of the house was about two feet deep, while inside it was only about half a foot deep. The next thing we knew, one of the French doors came crashing into the house, followed shortly by the back door bowing, and being pushed out by the rapidly rising water filled with leaves and mud. At that time, we decided that we had to abandon our house and go over to the Bed and Breakfast (Woodland Oaks Inn), my parent's house, which is next door to our house, about 30 yards away. It is on higher ground and is built on 24 inch piers.

The whole family, including Frank and I, three dogs, and four children, waded over to the Bed and Breakfast in waist deep water, against the current. One of the twins, John, had his pillow over his shoulder. I was afraid he would be swept away soon, if he continued to have this pillow dragging in the water. He let it go, and later we found it across the street. When we got to the Bed and Breakfast, the water was just over the wood floors. I grabbed some blankets, pillows, canned food, a can opener, and the ice tray out of the refrigerator and climbed up into the attic with the kids. Frank started putting things up to escape the rising water, while trying to monitor it. We put the dogs on the mattresses, but they weighed too much and began to sink. So, Frank carried them up into the attic, too, and then he just sat there on the pull-down attic steps and watched as the water continued to rise.

Up in the attic, there was a lot of praying going on. I was worn out from carrying a dog under my arm, although he dog paddled most of the way. The first thing I did in the attic was to pull off one of the aluminum strips on the vent at the end of the roof. It came off easily and so did the screen. I just wanted to make sure we could get out if we had to. I didn't know when the water would stop.

Finally, when the water was just below the window sills, it stopped rising and began to recede. Frank made sure the doors were open so the water could get out of the house. It wasn't long until it had gone down enough that we were able to get back over to our house to survey the damage.

It looked like someone had shaken our house and made all the furniture move and tumble. The smell was bad and the mud, the kind that sticks to your shoes till you have Paul Bunyan size feet, was all over everything. The water had gotten up to six feet in our house.

We were like drowned mice, except not dead, and there was nothing to drink or eat. We felt helpless. The funny thing is, I never thought about what the rest of the Coast must have looked like. I just thought about what our street had suffered.

We drove to Jackson, the state capital, around 7:30 the night of the hurricane. A two and a half hour drive took us six hours of dodging downed trees and debris. No one was traveling south, except for a convoy of National Guardsmen from Camp Shelby, and some highway patrol and other authorities.

We bought a generator, Shopvac, dehumidifier, pressure washer, chain saw, and lots of cleaning supplies. Two weeks after the storm, we drove down in our new RV, which we bought to live in, to clean up and recover what we could. We had some friends from Maryland who came down and brought us clothes and food, and they worked hard cleaning up our house and the Bed and Breakfast. They are the reason we are living in the Bed and Breakfast right now. We will always be grateful to them. A special thanks to Skip and Joyce Morgan and Joyce's son, Thomas.

This is not the end of the story. It may never end. There are many folks with the same story as mine, some with a tragic end. We realized what was really important in this life. It was a wake up call to me. I will treasure life more and not things. You can replace most things and you sure can't take it with you.

After

Before

29

Connie Heitzmann

They say teachers – true teachers – never retire. They just find new ways to teach. Connie Heitzmann has taken that to a new level. What was once a classroom experience for her Kindergarten students has become a treat for children of all ages.

In August of 2005, Connie had just begun her 33rd year of teaching Kindergarten at Bay Catholic Elementary in Bay St. Louis, Mississippi when Hurricane Katrina hit. The storm not only caused great damage to the school, but destroyed Heitzmann's house. Out of a desperate situation, Connie once again found a way to continue her life's work of bringing joy and learning to children of all ages. She has often been heard to say, "Although Katrina took my house, it did not take my home, and certainly not my spirit."

A recipient of Honor Recognition of Disney Teachers of the Year 2006, Connie now uses her many talents to bring to life lively characters that capture the imagination of children. Through storytelling, dance, art, and literature, Connie encourages the kids to set their imaginations free as they learn respect, tolerance, and acceptance. Even the most timid come to life with Connie in the room.

A lifelong resident of her beloved Bay St. Louis, Mississippi, on the Mississippi Gulf Coast, Connie has been married to her husband, Bob, for 39 years. They have one son, Matt, and recently welcomed daughter-in-law, Ashley, to the family.

by Betsy Gagnet

Connie

Eye of Katrina
"My Moat Broke"
Critter Queen Castle

Special thanks and love to all of our Family of Volunteers. This includes all family, friends, neighbors, the Camero family, Stacy Spangler and crew, Richard Killiam and crew, Dottie Scheurbaum and crew, Susan Wiseman and crew, Jill Sterrett, Grey Sterrett and crew, and all public servants. Also, many miracles happened with the greatness of our beloved Salvation Army, Red Cross, and faith-based groups. Thanks to Anderson Cooper, Kathy Koch, Robin Roberts, Shepard Smith, and the many local, national, and international news crews.

Their tireless efforts will be appreciated for all the years to come. Our additional thanks goes out to our Alaskan friends, our friends from France, and especially YOU!

Index of Artists

Freckles the Firefly is the design of Janie Koch.
Small Coast Critters seen on many pages are creations of Sylvia Corban and Janie Koch.

Co-author Connie Heitzmann (Project Visionary) is available for book readings, musical storytelling, and creative adventures in time.

Connie Heitzmann, P.O. Box 2206, Bay Saint Louis, MS 39520
Or call her at: 1.228.467.1892

To order additional copies of this book, please contact either:

Connie Heitzmann, P.O. Box 2206, Bay Saint Louis, MS 39520
Or call her at: 1.228.467.1892

Janie Koch, 23095 Woodland Way, Pass Christian, MS 39571
Or call her at: 1.228.452.3266

We'd love to hear from you!